THE AFTERLIFE IS A DRY COUNTY

For Eileen

Chauni Alice Hem

The Afterlife is a Dry County

ISBN: 978-1-937806-01-9

© 2011, Charmi Keranen

Big Wonderful Press, LLC.

Brooklyn, NY

All Rights Reserved.

Acknowledgements:

Poems in this manuscript have appeared or will be forthcoming in *The Salt River Review, JMWW, Stirring, blossombones, The Dirty Napkin, Passages North, Ouroboros Review, Inter\rupture* and *Grasslimb Journal.*

CONTENTS

Native America(n)	7
And What of the Moss	8
Tua Pulchra Puella	9
Däk-Bungalow	10
The Afterlife is a Dry County	11
The Great American Interchange	12
The Center for Wooden Boats	13
Gulping it Down	14
Late Cretaceous	15
Deer-Dusk of an Evening	17
Seney	18
A Treaty of Everlasting	20
A New Mythology	21
Low Ceilings	22
The Well-Tempered Clavicle	23
The Teeth of my Existence are Buried in the Wall	24
Leon Gambetta Flees Paris in a Balloon	25
The South Shore	27

Native America(n)

Sherman Alexie prefers to be
called an Indian, but still...

I take the word
Indian in my mouth, explore

Its curves with my white
woman tongue

Incorrigible cream & fall out
on the banks of the Baugo

Osceola, Indiana
into August

Land of the Indians
sans a single one

Seven one-legged egrets
eye a chainsaw

leaning against a willow

We've come here together

The fatalistic wood

And What Of The Moss

The couple you saw
lying deep inside themselves

their backs pressed into
that tall blue field

their hands touching

the grass and its sway

There was a stolen bicycle chained
to a crucifix

The Born Again don't bleed

or pedal — really

I looked, once, into
those gray polished stones

The woman's lips were moving

The man was closing his eyes

Tua Pulchra Puella

A man walks into a bar and says
to the waitress, *Tua pulchra
puella.* Slow, very slow. And
the waitress stares at him, just
stares at him. Because she knows
it isn't true. The weight of the language
is more than her waitress arms can bear.
But the man is flapping, frantically
flapping, on the head of a pin. No
angel, no wings, losing balance, not
sure where to begin. The waitress falls
over the horizon, an orbit, and circles
back again. The man quickly opens
his hand. *I'm holding five copper pennies*,
he says, then suddenly folds his palm.
What is the forbidden city, she asks
him, *and when can we go again.*

Däk-Bungalow

I know about the other room.

Daisy-cutter kissing wolf spider sliding eggs into a cast iron pan.

Except for you, and you.

Good morning, sunshine.

Touch the white of his back, the coldest parade.

I know halogen blue nipples,

calumet isn't a city,

the wind doesn't chime.

The Afterlife is a Dry County

He refuses to call them
structural.

Stair-step cracks, cold in
the grasp, stippling.

The vertebrae

lingering
whatever alludes

a prescient motion.

I watched a woman with the
mind of a bison light up a foyer.

This is my fault, isn't it.

The deep wet felt,

the undertow.

The Great American Interchange

The woman in the leopard print dress
Wants you to believe

It's all natural

The American lion much larger
13,000 years ago

(and living)

Long legs parting

The American Serengeti

Great gods of evolution!

(and silicone)

I believe—

In extinction

In the futility of calling
God good *in the particular*

(or of calling)

In the wireless clicking of the centipede

The Center for Wooden Boats

Alligator gar crawling
beneath her skin

It's akin to suturing
cobwebs to moonbeams

He's got an itch

Biting evolution

by a billion degrees

She only remembers waking up

Blue-etched keys
to a scratched limousine

I can separate everything

Alpaca touch at ten

Cherry wash at three

She stirs beneath the linens

He unzips
a dark telephoto lens

Gulping It Down

Seven times seventy I have
heard you tell of palming
the communion wafer during
the wedding of the semi-famous
Mr. and Mrs. You Know Who.
The priest stopped the ceremony,
chased your sorry ass to the last
row of the Basilica of the Sacred
Heart, demanded the return of
the body. You gulped it down,
then later hid in a coat closet.
I wish I could have been there
at that moment when the
god-flesh became your story,
instead of the other way around.

Late Cretaceous

1.

Say the hummingbird's a home wrecker

Spider-cropped or furious

How else to account for

The missing orbs

The white fields of porches

Heather filling the salvage yard

2.

My landlord is dying

The man in love with the idea
of being loved

Is building an igloo

Sewing morning glory into the seams

Such timing!

3.

The City of God segues into
The half-life of urban decay

100,000 years out from the homeland

We're still dreaming

Of a mother tongue or a passport

Something personal

To touch against our skin

Deer-Dusk Of An Evening

I take Mother's bones to town,
sell them to the lowest bidder,

pennies on the ounce. She calls
in the morning, inquiring about

her shoes, Grandmother's Cadillac,
other forms of abuse.

I unpin my hair and launch
a pineapple grenade.

Washington State phones.
Apologies for the trains.

Grandmother, surely, won't survive the ride.

A waterfall slices in behind the eye.

Cousin Jean's red Mustang
rots beneath pines.

The '51 Ford in the barn,
16,000 miles. No one ever

drives it. It's never been used.

Seney

It's slow going

waiting for the rock
to become a fish

the log
a grebe

the eagle's nest hovers
naked and known

but who in their right mind
would leave

the SUV to fight the deer flies

100,000 ticks per moose

*

We used a retractable razor blade
to scrape the inspection stickers

from each window carefully

safe for another year

yes, there was a forest fire

a virgin pine burn

then blue buckets of berries
all those following years

the town was skirted
like a woman

you're dying to surround

Hemingway said

The Big Two-Hearted

was more poetic

A Treaty of Everlasting

God might show up
Later

Today
Beside the river

I'm undressing our throes

You are pouring
Cold agate against a glass bowl

It's leaking

I am
More time than trembling

A basket of holding inside
A legion of siege

Tonight, god willing

We will flay mackerels

We will spit in the eyes of anemones

A New Mythology

It's not about the bees

We dream differently

Faces to the ground
listening for the thimble

in the water table
set for who knows who

It's flowing through
this earth and that earth

weaving the earths together
into a primordial ooze

This is a mythology
Who knows what is true

In my dreams you

are naked and bleeding
have three children

are a black butterfly

We argue

It's not about the bees

You are carving a cave
in the back of the moon

Low Ceilings

From Minneapolis to Frankfort

I want
To open the walls

Find bees in the borings
A long lost razor

A shaker of hail

The skeleton of a letter
Dear Thunder God

Struck through with honey
Crystallized bone

The afterlife stirring
In the bend of a finger

The absence of soil

The Well-Tempered Clavicle

I've got to get back to the
lisping lung, the feral staircase,

the malignant gray plank, the
lethal begun. That is to say,

your lips, beautifully pressed
silencers,

a convulsant chest wall.

The plumb line's a pendulum.

The Teeth of My Existence are Buried in the Wall

Smile for the camera

Or the coroner, whoever's next in line

Today, for instance, a 2-for-1 sale

Anesthesia & Contracts

Light gray shirts, charcoal pants,
charcoal jackets via the USPS

However…

*Pour visiter le veuve-cliquot.com
vous devez l'âge légal autorisé
 pour acheté ou consommer d'alcool*

Bien sûr

Sign on the dotted

List three close contacts

If it's of value, leave it behind

Leon Gambetta Flees Paris in a Balloon

5.

Flight 5970

On the very lips of your intended

      an aspirational cabal

Pink neon floating vacancy

The rope you're holding has torn
      the flesh from your palms

4.

Under mysterious circumstances
you have taken a room
near The Inn at Grinder's Stand

      (It's now a wheat field)

A woman is moaning

3.

A woman is always moaning

2.

You have drifted

Beyond the Alleghenies
They're closing

      the aboriginal lands

Sorry settlers!

This is the last call

1.

You fear fire and bodies of water

The weather is dry

A horse has lost itself in the forest

Leif Erickson has landed in L'Anse aux Meadow

The South Shore

Pack it, a taste of mule

The East Chicago man with an Egyptian jawbone
      And a Harley Davidson jacket

Opines across the aisle

She was too beautiful to be hooking

We're all too beautiful
To be on this train

The Notre Dame law students
Having a sidebar

My standard of living

No, ma'am, I don't have a pen or a pain killer

I have a 4x2 Japanese silk screen print
From the Art Institute that is teetering

Above my head all four seasons of fishes

And flowers in progression

The last stop is South Bend
      You won't miss it

A long quietude